SOME OF US LOVE YOU

RARE BIRD
Los Angeles, Calif.

SOME OF US LOVE YOU

RYAN KENT AND BRETT LLOYD

THIS IS A GENUINE RARE BIRD BOOK
PUBLISHED IN ALLIANCE WITH DEAD BOOKS PUBLISHING

Rare Bird Books
453 South Spring Street, Suite 302
Los Angeles, CA 90013
rarebirdlit.com

Cover Artwork by Diogo Soares

FIRST TRADE PAPERBACK ORIGINAL EDITION

Rare Bird Books Subsidiary Rights Department
453 South Spring Street, Suite 302
Los Angeles, CA 90013

Set in Dante
Printed in the United States

10 9 8 7 6 5 4 3 2 1

Publisher's Cataloging-in-Publication Data available upon request.

RYAN KENT

RYAN KENT is the author of three collections of poetry: *Hit Me When I'm Pretty*, *This Is Why I Am Insane*, and *Poems For Dead People*. He is the microphone player for the thrash band Murdersome, and contributes to Ozy.com and *RVA Magazine*. He lives Cali-sober in Richmond, Virginia.

Thank you to my family, to loved ones, and to the people who taught me to write.

BRING ME MY MONSTER

i go to the park for peace sometimes
sit on an open bench overlooking the city
smoking cigarettes

i can write here
until a boombox gets turned on
people start having a good time
which happens

a lady is using one of the
park's free exercise machines
it works like a runner works
each leg has to push
              from the hip
            down

            through the femur
            to the knee
            through the tibia
            to the ankle
when you get the thing in a rolling motion
the centrifugal force will keep it going
as long as you keep pushing

in theory you could go on forever

i look up and the lady is gone
a neighborhood kid is there instead
moving the machine with rubber legs

i look down to write
look up again
now he's gone

w a i t   there he is
            halfway up the hill
              behind the machine
screaming   bring me my monster
the machine is still moving

i look at the news for a while
the big men are saying big things again
using fingers like they are only
meant to be pointed
they've really done it this time
i put the news away   look at the cityscape
the sun has pushed down the horizon
someone turns on a boombox
people start having a good time
which happens
peace doesn't last forever
bring me my monster   he said
don't worry kid
it's coming

ATLAS

he doesn't wear a wristwatch
he doesn't go fishing or for walks
the grass is cut the car is washed
but you don't see him do either

embassy bombs are going off in baghdad
people are sick all over the place
astronomers found molecular oxygen
581 million light years away

the old man probably doesn't
have the newspaper delivered
still uses a drum
to telephone

he's leaned in a kitchen chair
by the shed out west of the house
whistling that one ben selvin tune
because he's figured it out

how to live in this world
but away from it

on two legs

SIT HERE AND DIE

on campus in the business building
second floor all the way in the back
        a room
        like a big storage closet
you could smoke cigarettes in there all day
oscillating fans pushed the smoke around
        sun came through the window
        like a deity
all i wanted to do
was sit in there
cigarette after cigarette
nobody bothered me
it was quiet
like you don't interrupt a man
who's pissing or praying quiet
i've smoked in nicer rooms since then
but it was never the same
listen to people talk enough
you'll appreciate the quiet
the peace

how nice it is
that's all i'm asking for
not even heaven

PAPER TRAIL

he'd take me with him
the place wasn't called   bill's
even though two old men named bill
operated it
each wore a lab coat over their shirt
had haircuts like george jones
and the only white collars in the room
occasionally there'd be a wait
some local man seated in the chair
beer belly burial mound under the smock
a few pumps up on the foot pedal

talking all kinds of quiet nothing
one of the bills would be clipping
the hairs on the man's neck with
boot camp style wahl seniors
gray hairs
like metal filings
like paratroopers
old-timers came in without
appointments or enough hair
to run a comb through
maybe just to get away
from something worse than baldness
the younger of the bills choked on a chicken bone
i don't know what happened to the other one
sometimes you get so old you disappear

they tell you not to get greedy
not to leave a paper trail
if you become a criminal or a christian
the bill who choked
knew when it was quitting time
just hand me my shit
and let me get out of here

THEN THE BABY CAME

i found coffee on the first floor
when i got back upstairs
the waiting room was empty
an episode of fix some house
was repeating on the tv
i soft tapped on the office glass
asked the receptionist if she
could please mute the volume
she did this just as

a baby began to cry
down the hall
but this time
it wasn't about
the alabaster

ALMOST DONE

the thing i like about birds
they don't speak english
unless they speak english in bird
they do it all day with gusto
i can't understand it
but i like how it sounds
drive over to a small café
young people take up all the tables
talking all day and saying nothing
i don't remember being like them
their words are safe and popular
their gusto sucks
                    i buy the coffee i came for
                 i go back to where i came from
the neighbor's maine coon
is moving across my lawn
as i pull into the driveway
it's raining and the sun is going down
the birds are now singing
the same verse out of order
i watch the cat pluck a soprano
from the hedge by the front window
to sing it something entirely different

$90 AND A HARD-ON

he was usually unshaven
wind tunnel overcast hair
new england accent
introduced himself as   m a h k
wore secondhand clothes
had dumb teeth
bad tattoos
                    drove a worn out
          o l d s m o b i l e
entry level
computer data job
mark
he smoked dope in a pipe
with a   s k u l l   on it
in a basement apartment
off seminary road
still had a   g r a f f i x   bong
named his dog   g r a f f i x   bong
he'd walk into the bar
start sending people rail shots
                    we were all lonely
mark had
this side hustle
doing studies in a tall building
d own t own
              he'd have to apply
              a weird oil to his neck
              watch porn   or
              battle footage   or
              an old broadcast
              of the berlin wall
              coming down

              while some intern measured
              his heart rate and asked him
              what he thought
              about america

14

after each visit
they'd cut him a check
if he came into the bar
smelling weird
you knew he had
$90 and a hard-on
one afternoon he came in
talking about the people in the building
d own t own
said he'd
figured them out
the way they finish us off
he said
        is by the sense of smell
television
movies
corporate music
sport utility vehicles
inflatable bodies
fad foods
they've already got us with those
he said
but real mind control
is done with
our noses
bullshit
said the bartender
i swear
to god

i'm not making this up
mark said
it'll be on a necklace
a pendant
a 15-second commercial
will air once during the super bowl
within 96 hours
pendants will be hanging around the necks
of every suburban family in the midwest

no more driver's licenses
social security cards
birth certificates
bank accounts
policy numbers
your personal data
is stored in that pendant
on that necklace
your blood type
your fingerprints
your dental records
your credit score
your mother's maiden name
etcetera
once it's adopted by celebrities
it'll spread like an oil spill
he held up a coin
it's a calming disc
                    that looks like a nickel
                    said   the bartender
fuck you joe
said mark
he placed the coin
on the bar
                    it's the size of
                a lithium battery
                        he said
        it puts off
    a unique smell
per individual
a pheromone
or something like one
it relieves
neuro ailments
sensory ailments
c h r o n i c
p ai n
you no longer take a pill
for anything   ever

they'll kill off big pharma
    for us

the disc
in the pendant
will change
e v e r y t h i n g
it'll unite
the people
we'll trust   th em
again
like we did
with   f d r
that ben selvin tune
will come back with bells on
war won't seem so   b ad
taxes won't seem so   ba d
people won't have savings
their money is spent

sedating
groceries delivered to homes
the newest devices and
beauty products and eyewear
shoes of the month fold up
home s   and
           microcar s
delivered   anywhere
art and   s e x
and dreams and dru g   s
just as long as you're
               wearing that goddamn pendant
  they're yours
     & then
            entry level
            computer data job
            mark   s a i d
  they're
  go n n a   eat us

it got bad tip quiet
a few guys turned
around in their stools
the bartender brought mark
the shots and his tab
i took one of the shots
then another
mark didn't bother me
i liked his story
it was something to
                    hear

                              we were all lonely
after that
i went home
lit a candle

                         put olive oil
                         on my neck
watched some   p o r n
some battle footage

and an old broadcast
of the
            b e r l i n
            w a l l
             com
              ing
              d
             o
         w
             n

DYING COMES WITH AGE

i do this out of desperation mostly
and it feels like you'd imagine
i thought i'd be a priest or a monk
or an entirely different kind of father
sit in one place long enough and
you can talk yourself out of anything
so you find something like this
to distract yourself from something like that
most of the time people find it
watching what other people are doing
i guess you can't put the groceries away
and sweep the floor every night
people have lost their minds
over a lot more and a lot less
watch how the sun dries out
the fly parts on the window ledge
the wings and legs and heads
after a while life repeats itself
and it works best when you're not
holding your breath

EVERYDAY LIFE IS MADNESS

i was sitting on a concrete slab
behind a coffee shop smoking a cig
two men were walking down the alley
both had backpacks and winter coats
tread worn reeboks giveaway hats
brown paper bag amber dreams
we exchanged glances
they stopped behind a dumpster
twisted the tops off the paper bags
took healthy pulls from the easy cheap

god   how they smiled
i was jealous

SET FOR STUN

when i see my parents now
they remind me what will be mine after they die
padding around the living room pointing at
this and this   don't you just love this
after dinner she tells me the table and chairs
her grandmother's silver
and all the plates and glassware will also belong to me
my father's way is different than my mother's
less formality fewer words
reminds me with a twirl of his finger
which loafs from thing to thing for him
their divorce was finalized 35 years ago
it has trailed each of us like a dead kid
we don't interrupt visits anymore with stale talk
but you can still smell the words
there are bridges and crowns and partials now
and we're all waiting closed mouthed
for god to bite down
to prove that every bit of this is gold

PAYING ATTENTION

she drove an acura tl
the trunk was held down
by two bungee cords
she was held down by none
nosing the car's bumper
closer
c l o ser
c l o s e r

to my bumper at 45
in a school zone
her face in the rearview
was blank
unconscious
dead eyed
i waved her on
she
gave me the finger
shouted
            vividly
f u c k y o u
her face contorted
venomous
mid strike
she coiled
around traffic

no signal
to her patterns
most animals
give you a
warning to show
their intent
a rattle
or bared teeth or
chest beating
before they lunge
the animals today

22

give no such
consideration
i pulled back onto the road
got back up to the speed limit

missed my turn
glad it
wasn't a
s
  n
a
  k
e

SAME AS IT EVER WAS

i used to go to the school
nurse's
            office a lot
she'd check my
temperature
tell me to go lie down
on one
of the
                patent leather beds
i'd pull the privacy curtain
                        all the way
a   r   o
d   n   u
there with my hands folded beneath my ear
trying to guess how long she'd let me stay
before sending me   b a c k
as the phone rannnnngggggggg
and
other pretenders
            pulsed))))))) in to have their
t e m p e r a t u r e s
                taken also
i liked it in the nurse's office
                i don't know why

i liked sad songs
and newyorkcity
                m a y b e
it had something to do with that
back then we got bullied by the bigger boys
and now we get bullied by the bigger nerds
and there are a lot of pretend nerds
in newyorkcity
s o   here's a sour apple
to keep the doctor   a w a y

24

I DON'T HAVE ANY OF THE ANSWERS

it was the day after
graduation
i drove down to
ebb tide beach
two rednecks sat at the end of the pier
passing a bottle of port wine
a skinny one
a fat one
and an afternoon orioles game
losing signal on a transistor radio
i went to the opposite side
to cast out my line
chuck thompson described ripken's stance
when something hit my bait
i reeled it in
a perch hooked
center through the belly
the fat one stood up on its hind legs
what'd ya git
           he asked
a little one
               i said
he stumbled over
reached a paw out for the fish
looked at it
ah man
that's a fatal injury
               he said
this was true
he unhooked
the fish
dropped
it to the pier
stepped
on it hard
pink and white
s p r e a d   o u t

jesus
         i said
he tried to make
the sign of the cross
wobbled back over
to the skinny one and the radio
i sat down on
the edge
looked out over
the water
ripken trotted
back to the dugout
now that i think about it
the fat one was right

THE PRICE WE PAY

hemingway found a way out
he didn't put on paper

hunter used the same strategy
dylan thomas went with booze
plath and sexton hit the gas
people spoke of each
critically after they
died
maybe
to bargain
their own intellect
to the people
bargain
        an agreement to exchange goods
        at a price
last month
people took down
my reading posters
before the date
advertised
replaced them
with their own posters
ten years
before that
someone shimmied
w a y u p
on a light pole
removed
my band's sticker
the only sticker
from its spot
stuck their band sticker
in its place instead
somebody
always thinks
their thing is better

than your thing
their music
their ethos
their diet
whatever
i read hemingway and hunter
i read dylan thomas
plath and sexton
you kids can't
take them
down
what a bargain

THANKS FOR THE LINE NEIL

he told me my poems needed lions
i don't know what the man wanted from me
twelve years later i can still hear these lions
making the same grunting noises
the thing about big cats is they always
go for where the voice lives
you don't hear much else about them
they only manage to eat and breed
worse are those that follow the lions
for what they drop
they're everywhere now
the skies have vultures
the oceans have sharks
the cities have werewolves
                              and
                              poets
this is my rifle
helping to keep
the population down
DON DELILLO
track rabbit
that's what they call rats
in the underworld of the subway system
the rats eat the other rats who have died
and in turn men who live down there
sometimes kill the rats to eat them
if you pay enough attention
you can find a pattern scratching in anything
might not be what you want to take home
but it's pumping blood nonetheless
rats eating rats
and men eating rats in the
train tunnels of new york city
most people ignore patterns
the size shape and frequency of what's
shining a flashlight at them
they choose state flowers

and chess pieces and wall street
pinecones and lunar moths
the pointing fingers of politicos
and   poetic   f o r m
rats giving birth to rats
hail mary full of grace
but people don't want to read
about rats on the sabbath
or the solitary men who live
down there in the graffiti
who have eaten rats on purpose
if you pay enough attention
you can find a pattern scratching in anything
track rabbit
that's what they call rats
in the underworld of the subway system

I KNOW WHAT LOVE IS

cookie
he called her cookie
i heard him yell it at her
like mayday through my ceiling
cookie this
cookie that
cookie cookie cookie
down the stairs   cookie
out the building door   cookie
if he'd blown a ref's whistle each time
he yelled cookie i'd have shot
the three of us
cookie cookie cookie cookie
goddamnit cookie
i saw her run across the street
he was shouting cookie from the
upstairs window of the apartment
he ran down after her
but i don't know if he ever
got cookie to come back
the city demolished that building
a few years ago   n o w
some other building is there
i think about cookie tonight
as i drive by the old address
wonder if she ever got away
when i get home
the woman is asleep
in bed with our two dogs
there's a lamp on
i turn it off

love is
quiet

READY FOR MY CLOSEUP MR DEMILLE

in bed
watching old
kung fu movies
the mosquitoes
are bad outside
a man
kicks people around
with karate
&   i like it
 evil   doers
            flyyyyyyyyyyyyyyyyyy
      into chairs
onto tables
            through plate glass
                              out   windows
no one smiles
a mosquito
has gotten into my room
                        she flies by the
                        burman lamp
                        on the night
                                stand
lands on the shade
            i know what she wants
      and she'll most likely
go for it sooner or later
and i think of the others
full of all that blood
                  who went for it
each one cried into my ear
in each of my different rented rooms
their   xxxxxxs
had different
         names   and different cocks
but i
was no
different   than their xxxxxxs
and

32

each told me so
which was the truth
        i didn't love them
i'm sorry i'd say
        i've wasted your time
on the vizio
    two men
      walk a path
        together
one says
        i do not hit
        it hits by itself
i go shower
pull nose hairs clip nails roll deodorant
brush teeth shave neck look in the mirror
no one smiles
                i go back to bed
she's still on the
lampshade
all right miss
i'm   r e a d y

THE BEE'S KNEES

in 1991 he handed me some tweezers
told me to go out into the yard
bring back a honeybee
i did this
told me to sting him on the knee
he said goddamnit
after i stung him
but it was a good
goddamnit
the honeybee prayed its hands together on
the sidewalk while my grandfather
said he'd read in the national enquirer
glucocorticoids helped soothe arthritis
and the bee stings would numb his knees
i got him another honeybee

he said goddamnit
after i stung him
but it was a good
goddamnit
things were different in 1991
saying goddamnit meant something
like the end of pain or beginning of it
i don't know what it means
do you

A BUNCH OF HOOEY

blue was my favorite as a kid
i don't know why
maybe because my mother
dressed me in it often

maybe it was the sky or the bottom
of the swimming pool or the donald duck
fishing pole i fished with and the color was
just an association with those things
jennifer told me tonight
you will be dead in 2–4 months
a paint by numbers kind of cancer
i point out the blue and mention my mother
because you were married to her for 26 years
i was writing this poem and hit a snag
right after the part about the fishing pole
then jennifer told me about the cancer
with writing as well as fishing
have patience with the snag
get it untangled   cast out the line
maybe bring home something blue

PUT IT IN THE DRAWER WITH THE REST

i saw a book outside
laying a little off the curb
it had been rained on run over
blown open in the middle
left there for
the morning crows
a kid on a bicycle stopped
picked up the book with two fingers
it looked like a dead
seagull held there
he saw me having
a pall mall on my porch
who the fuck is zane grey   he asked
a dentist   i said
no way
this looks like a cowboy book

doc holliday was a dentist   i said
he didn't seem
to know that name either
can i have one of those
cigarettes
no   i said
the kid dropped the book
pedaled down the street
lit one of his own
cigarettes
i hope none of mine
end up like that
keep them stiff on a shelf
next to your mother's ashes

82 BILLION BILLION GALLONS

i liked to piss in the atlantic
right through my jean shorts
it'd get warmer around me
an odd pride
there now
a good feeling
high tide rolling
my yellow remix
down 39 boards
into the pins of
a hairy back
my grandfather belonged
to a bowling league
as an extension
of his patriotism

had trophies in the attic
with little gold men on top
who'd been holding their balls
since eisenhower
i've seen other bowling trophies
in alleys and curio shops
all having similar gilded poses
old-timers waxing on in an old-timer bar
about bob perry being the best bowler
to ever wash out of new jersey
i push open the door to the commode
something's pooled on the floor
carved into the drywall above
the american standard it says
the world is your urinal
pissing in the atlantic doesn't matter
neither does bowling or eisenhower
the water only gets warmer for a moment
an odd pride there now
a good feeling

BANG

i smoke cigarettes
like shotguns in my mouth
but maybe it won't be so violent
maybe only hospice
or asphyxiation
before the payoff
yet still the chance of something so bad
i'll wish i'd never done it
a blindfolded man
stands before the firing squad
pall mall smoking between his lips
used as punctuation at the end of the line

sensing the slender arm of death
at his side
he'll say
i guess you must be the guy
or something far less
dignified

THE SKY IS FALLING

back   farther back   even farther back
let it fly
or tear its meniscus
nothing really knows
where it's going
what it's doing

it's just going
doing
could nosedive into a field somewhere
an hour before sunrise
or land hard against the shoulder of an unbuttoned
orthopedic surgeon in business class
pretzels   gin and tonic
conversation that drops with the air pressure
anyone telling you
any different isn't a pilot
people pretend to know
who they are
where they're going
the trajectory of a slingshot
their torn meniscus their tray tables
pretzels   gin and tonic

conversation that drops out of the sky
back   farther back   even farther back
i'll let you go if you let me go
a plane shooting across the horizon
could nosedive into a field somewhere
an hour before sunrise
anyone telling you
any different isn't a pilot

I'M DYING HOW ARE YOU

went in there
sat next to the bed
nurse said it wouldn't be long
most of him sat up
to look at me
said my name
i didn't say anything
what was there to say
he laid back down
nurse was right

THE HISTORY OF DOGS

i can't be around people much anymore
they look at me like i'm astray
down the sidewalk i asked myself again
why the hell do i keep going outside
i never know how to answer this
an old lady in front of the thai place
said my coat didn't look warm
the old guy with her called me buddy
but that's not my name

and I'm not his buddy
they kept looking at me funny
so i started running
sometimes i start running
with no idea where i'm going
and sometimes when i'm running
i think about running
right into the street
without looking both ways
hoping no one is around
to see if i make it
to the other side
of that which
has led me
there

DRAW BLOOD

she asked you not to shut the bedroom door
lester shut the door before he shot himself
you said you wouldn't shut the bedroom door
people like to tell you who you are
tell other people who you are
chew up your identity
they will never stop doing this
they love you
k i   crooked letter
                    crooked letter
                                teeth
after long enough you say   no
no   you're mistaken   that's not who i am
but they can't hear you
not over all the crooked letters and teeth

a closed door is exactly what it is
there's peace in hearing something clap
behind you
it's over for now
how nice

I MADE MY FAMILY DISAPPEAR

it didn't take much
but one by one
they were gone
smelling salts can wake
a fighter from the cold
yet this snowfall
provided no cut man
no corner

bell rung
dukes dropped
out on my boots
wandering the canvas
90 degrees above
h o r i z o n t a l
old trainers say
good fighters never develop
the f l i g h t instinct
they lean into the pain
instead of turning away
the body can take
what the head cannot
jostle the hippocampus
maybe you'll remember things
like your grandmother's
chipped lateral incisor
uncle bobby's wooden leg
boxing day is canadian
i've been hit a lot
i lean into the pain
but i'm not a good fighter
can't see but i can remember
the faces the smokey mouths
meat eaters and drinkers
good fighters don't turn away from danger
but i'm not a good fighter
it's a learned behavior

you don't have to see them
to remember
it's never ever heaven honey
just winter

LESSONS IN SHAVING

i don't remember what i was thinking
about while shaving this morning
i know it wasn't about the razor
or the water or the hair in the sink
together again in that order
this was something thicker
now down the drain congealed
around god knows what

she had nice handwriting
also nice taste in furniture and decorations
she looked good with a bald head
she was a good mother

i used the stretch mark lotion
from the medicine cabinet
applied some to the neck areas that bump
scratching off charcoal toothpaste spots
dalmatianed across the mirror

she was careful with her opinions
also careful not to follow anything blindly
she respected art more than people
she was loved by her mexican street dogs

i should've bought a new razor after
the last time i shaved
i do that with everything
i procrastinate i bargain i deal

one last shave and then another
and then one more and then
fuck it until there's rust
or the blade is too dull

she had tattoos in her armpits
and you could just see the little hairs
she liked to mow the grass after it rained
she always had weed and a can of gasoline

it's been six months

she drank hot tea from handmade mugs
she had good music to her laugh
she read tarot but had good sense
she gave money to men in the median

driving helps this
coffee and cigarettes helps this
if there's an empty park somewhere
that also helps this

she knew how to frame a photo
she was good at giving gifts
she gave them sans holiday
she dropped everything in the kitchen

avoiding phone calls is wise
people still use answering machines
nothing's dire unless the hinges
are being taken off your door

she liked having the porch windows open
she liked burning fake fire logs
she liked nag champa
and the song   joey

when it rains at night in the summer
the mosquitoes find an open bar
you can sit outside watching cars pass
spinning the world on its axis

the rain softens everything

if the wind doesn't blow too much
you can see steam from the asphalt
find its way to god

people think if you leave someone
you are happy to be gone

i feel sorry for those people

going is leaving is ending is dying
but nothing outside of this will stop spinning
you must keep buying razors

or maybe   just tell yourself that
or something else like it

HOOP DREAMS

ethel used to live up the street
jim said he went out with her once
said she made him try on all her
dead husband's shoes
said she had eleven cats in that apartment
sometimes a light would be on up there
ethel sitting around with all her cats
and all her dead husband's shoes
i don't think she ever remarried
but that's not to say she didn't think about it
she did go out with jim

NO MY GOD

having plenty of cigarettes always matters
also a lighter or another way to make fire
this is how i learned to pray
nights of madness days spent reading
necessary intermittent smoke breaks
portioned out like dolmades are
portioned out like sedatives are
drive somewhere for dinner
smoking is prohibited in zorba's
the old liturgy of heathen gods
is now observed out of doors
xanax
zan axe
zen acts
take divinity as needed with water
the other tables try
to pronounce gyro
jai ro   guy ro   gee ro
hee ro   yee ro
pointing their fingers
speaking mostly in vowels
sounding out the consonants
like dinner lambs
g e e   w h y   a r e   o h
zen acts
zan axe
xanax
take divinity as needed with water
god showed us once for free
even had it chipped into stone
then left us alone for 3500 years to think about it

THE SET

i watched him cut the backyard
with an old motorless push mower
just two wheels and a length of blade
pushed it around the trampoline and
over the thick patch beneath the magnolia
where grass had grown to the knee
it started to rain
didn't get much done   he said
pulling the mower behind him
i forget about the backyard
he reached into the cooler for a beer
caught his breath under the porch ceiling
even with the rain coming down hard
it was easy to point out where he'd left off
what about all that over there   i pointed

by august it'll be burnt up anyway
i'll just come out here with a sickle

do you own a sickle
somebody does   he said
water began to fill in the fire pit
and other various holes in the yard
i can do things like that now   he said
let the grass get real high
hack it down with a sickle
the city will fine you   i said
for the sickle
for the grass   i said

there's a privacy fence
with large gaps in parts   i said
i'll nail up some plywood   he said
we continued to watch the rain
the neighbor's dogs barked at
the other neighbor's dogs
it's still a nice place   i said
it'll be nicer when everything's unpacked

doesn't look like you packed much
just clothes and some lamps   he said
what's to unpack
those things   he said
where are you gonna sleep
i got a bed coming friday
is it part of a set
mattress and box spring only
i guess she took the set
neither of us took the set   he said
movers left it on the curb
i would've taken the set
you already have a set   he said
doesn't matter
what would you have done with another set

given it to someone   i said
who
i don't know   i said
since i don't have the set
probably still out there   he said
chucking the empty bottle at the trampoline
it's been rained on now   i said
a vein opened in the sky
the clouds reached down
thunder clapped so loud it'd make you
disregard the devil
suit yourself   he said
it stopped raining a half hour after that
later on i drove across town
to see if the set was still out there
the landlord had the nightstands in his truck
asked me if i wanted the set
said the city was gonna fine him
if it wasn't all gone by friday

THE TIMES OF OUR WIVES

people finally moved into the house
across the street with the tin roof
lights were on even during the daytime
they were drinkers
the one they called russ
was sprawled out in the middle of the yard
shouting w h o r e s over and over
holding on to that big belly of his
his wife came out there in a nightgown
knelt in the grass beside him
put her hand on his cheek
said something soft
you're all whores   he shouted
the neighbors turned on their porch light
a few dogs started barking
w h o r e s   he shouted again
more dogs started barking
she walked back inside
shut the motion light off
russ lay there still holding his big belly
you're all   w h o r e s

i could hear the toilet running again
i went in to jiggle the handle
poured a cup of cold coffee
came back out
cops were talking to russ
he'd stopped shouting
shit himself   one of the cops said
i lit a cigarette
feeling it my civic duty
to witness how this transpired

PETER YOU'VE BECOME A PIRATE

i've spent these years burying things
people change with the tide to forget
who they were all those other times
you can't escape who you've shaken with
oh darling just read between the lines
of my hook hand
fall through these invisible fingers
like jolly ranchers
jolly rogers
the yak hairs of my
black candle wig
darling i forget
we were kids once
who is this old man
i see now in the deep water
reflecting on all the smoke
he's s h o t g u n n e d
into every
single chest
he's left here
for you

HELL AND SKY

i'll move this day over with the others dear
we're not looking at the same horizon anymore
you're looking at ponies and sunshine
i don't even know what i'm looking at
if they send me back again dear
maybe it'll be as something different
a maple tree or one of those ponies
maybe a caterpillar mother
a single barrel a double barrel
or maybe just another man
when the sun goes blind
and the darkness comes to
remind you where you really are
extend those fingers
when you reach down
to say
o hell
hell o
again
dear

SISTER INCREDIBLE

darlene with the crooked teeth
she was incredible
yvonne and her muddy jeep
incredible
louise jumping horses
christine and her divorces
all of them were incredible
nelle was a seamstress
adele moved back east
clara said belle bought the farm
martha mary elizabeth
another mary
incredible
every
one
rose wasn't named after a flower
candy wasn't after something sweet
sarah had a stolen rolex
tiffany also drove a jeep
sabrina cut my heart out
and frances fanned the flame
but the sister who set the table
i won't list her
here by name
i never spoke to
more than half of them
not a single one was ever mine
but all of them
i n c r e d i b l e
or maybe just
divine

BRETT LLOYD

BRETT LLOYD is a native of Virginia Beach. He is the author of *Deception of Change*, *Hateburn*, and *Hour of Man*, and is the frontman for Pillbuster, Mammoth Black, and Down Again.

Thank you to everyone for everything. You know who you are and you know who you are not.

We never know the importance until we walk away
The shaded glass grows darker as the image falls silently backward
Times never ending plow with our minds
You seem to underestimate the reasons
We together as one
Rolling around on the good times
Looking tired at the bad
Through it all, the remains of silence have cut me
And the blood still spills
Running out of my eyes
Down my face
Temptation lacks meaning
Truth runs red down my body
And onto your floor
You stand there guessing
Remembering
Falling down to your knees
Into my blood bath of emotion
Welcome quiet one
See the world of pain
How it draws your attention
Put down your broken shard of glass
Don't cut yourself
Let me do it
Let me be the one to make to make you realize what is happening
I want to shed the blood from your body

The stars hang low tonight
The moon shines through the skies of destruction
Rain washes it all away
The new day
The new pain
The cuts get deeper
The fresh blood looks good as it glistens to the touch of my tongue
The sands of time won't dry the sins
Laugh at me
Just once more
Spit at me
Just once more

And you'll find what you seek
Self-destruction looks good to you
Put the mask on
Now take the mask off
You look through different eyes because it gives you different reasons to
  hate yourself
I look through my eyes because they get new cuts everyday
You get to notice things after a while
Seeing though the blood and disarray
Carry on the thoughts of triumph
Lay down in my fluid of truth and understanding
I'm going to take pieces of you as a souvenir
I'm going to cut so deep into you that no one will recognize what you
  were before
We are going to live through this you and I
We will have a special bond unbreakable to ever be denied

◆ ◆ ◆

Good-bye yellow soldier
On a mountain of glass you stand
Looking at all the diamonds you once had in your hands
Throw it all away
Look at me
Give it all and take it all away
From yourself you learn how to fear
Because you fear the things other minds neglect to notice
Don't apologize to me
No way to get out this time
Just take it as it is
And find the way back home
Bring a shovel
Bring the wine
Find me when you get to the bottom

◆ ◆ ◆

In darkness I sit
Shrouded in black
Surrounded by walls that come closer and closer by the second

I look over at my candles
They start to flicker against my eyes
As though you're whispering into them, making the smoke spell your
    name
My body cries out for you
I know you need it to
I want to be the one to ease your pain
I close my eyes and open them to find your face staring into mine
I reach out to you
Can you feel me touch you
Your body goes against my lips
As I look into your eyes
I tend to get lost inside
Your movement brings me back
Temptation looking over my shoulder
I lay you on your back
Making you feel
How, I make you feel
I climb into you slowly
You try to catch your breath
I catch it for you
As I close my eyes I let my control rest for awhile
Your mind is racing
Your body screams
Emotion greets our every kiss
I back away from you now
So I can look at your body
I fall in love and climb back in
Your mind against mine
Slowly seeing each other's confusion
Slowly seeing the evolution as to what we have become
Time stands beside us
I look over at the hands that fate has dealt us
I close my eyes
To see if you still exist to me
After the pleasure has died
And we have exhausted all of our measures of understanding
And all of me and all of you have spilt all over these sheets
Who am I to you

♦♦♦

Sometimes I just stare at myself in the mirror
I'm not the same
Time claws down my back
Ripping skin
Eating flesh
Tearing me down
You were something I lacked
Something I wish I could hold forever
Hopes and dreams all dead into the wind
I wish I could say everything to you and that you would understand
But it's hard to talk with a gun in your mouth

♦♦♦

Good morning dawn
Your night eyes deceived by light
How long has it been since my burial
Hope has faded into a name I don't remember
I have selfish relations to death
Take my soul to Eve
Tell her I miss her breath on my skin
Take my mind to Dante
Let the flames dance high around my decisions
I died in vain always awaiting the kill
I wanted to destroy myself wearing the thorny crown of forgiveness
I wanted to play both sides
I wanted to see just how far I could go until I reached the end
Until I reached you, I've never seen the bottom before
Until now I've never known my equal
I'm glad we met

♦♦♦

Bleeding faces
Bleeding fear
Conformation of night
Bloody tears
Your face is etched on the wall in which you put your head against

An image of the past you will never forget
Did the world laugh at you
Tell you the lies you wanted to hear
As you walk away and look back do you see your world smeared
Has it climbed on top of you
Nestled on your stomach
Look you in the eyes
Please believe in something
But don't believe in their lies
I know you lie to yourself
You hide from the truth
Blind men always follow the blind
They scream at each other's windows
Is there someone outside
Does he have a knife
Does he want to cut out your pride
You run down the alleyways of dreams you've lost along the way
It's all a game of mindlessness
We pray you won't survive
As you sleep into tomorrow all of your yesterday's follow close behind
You can't erase the past
The road spikes are long
They dig into your feet
Come all the way up through your throat
Your body will soon dangle on a spike
You always thought it would be a rope
And the memories that are so new seem to bring you a new and justified
    pain
The blood rusts on your teeth
Stained
Emotion
Stained
Mind
Bleeding smiles and bleeding ears
You hear the screams echoing through the mind of neglect
You smile as you bleed ear to ear
You smell the dampness in your shirt
Your body tucks into a ball
Fire

Burning
Panting
Heart raping adolescence into the new culture of bred misunderstanding
A whole New world with death as a skin color
Invisible
Your eyes fall out of your skull
You pick them up with your tongue
Pulling it out to stretch the disease
Sanity is tossed out the window
The cracked faces smiling
Bleeding gums cracked to remember
Can you find the reasons to hate yourself
You can't go back to related personification
You lack what you truly feel
You dissolve into the fictitious world created by your cheap bravery of
    never understanding
The audience in which you place yourself in front of
I will eventually dissolve you
Into the ash that you are meant to be

♦♦♦

Blood is going to flow like a river tonight
There are so many questions
There's so much pain
I caused it
Indirectly but true
Intentional no but I can't stop but wonder
What everything will mean when the smoke is gone and we are left star-
    ring at each other
I wanted you
I needed you
I didn't even know you yet
Just the disguises that you pretend on the day to day
The messes you make and then you walk away
So what will we become
Now that the lines are drawn
That the wounds are fresh
That everything is left dead or alive in the moment gone

What will we be
Now that the wine has stained our tongue
That the music has overlapped
That the words and meaning and rhythm have declined to a steady trot
I stopped the music
I became the note after note
I hated the song
I hated the words
I hated myself
But most of all I began to hate you
Could you blame me
Look at me and the monster I've become
Tormented and dead to the forever you place me in

♦♦♦

Man stands in a field
Arms outstretched
Looking for salvation
Wanting the voices to quiet down
He wants to think about the past
About the voices inside his head
Life has nothing left to give him
He has taken so much
Spent it all
Died every fucking time

It's easy to die
We all want the taste
Just until you know…. The moment when
You pass over
To the new you
Fresh ideas
Slate clean
Some of us want it so bad.

♦♦♦

Life Reel
Do you see it coming down the street

Eyes closed
Gun in its mouth
Running from anything it can find
Except you
Because it runs through you
Under you
Crawling inside of you
Making the flames dance a little higher inside your soul
Making you fear it
Because it knows your true identity
And you thought knowing it was there would save you
Put you two steps ahead
Farther in front of existence
But you're just further behind than you think
Making you a target
But you were just a target anyway
With the mask you hide behind so well
So easy to fake it
So easy to think no one knows
That's when it grabs you
Reality
And the games continue to play
And the denial plagues every breath you take
Killing you slowly
Watching you die in its arms
While it breaks your flesh
So dry
So brittle
You stand alone
Spinning the thoughts
The dead memories
 The hate that burns your eyes when you see
The self-hate
Running
Punishing
Taunting you
While I have blood on my face
Blood on my hands
Blood running down my back

Choosing sides
Beating me down
Into a pile of bleeding flesh
Does it burn when it hits you
You don't like chewing on the barrel of a gun do you
You wish to end your fake deprived life of fear
Someone will find your plan and burn you
But you looked so good
In your brand new clothes
To fit your brand new identity
Was it fate that put the mask on
Was it fear
Was it me
Was it just fun to see the world play the game with you
I wasn't playing
Just watching you
Undress yourself for us
Claiming to taunt my desire
As you watch the men lick your thighs
Did it hurt more when I just stood there shaking my head
What did you want me to do
This is what you wanted isn't it
Was it pain or inspiration
Everything is ok
Everything is just fine
The more you scream in pain
The more they love you
Emotion makes a thick cloud
Reality makes a deep grave
For you to rest your lies in
For you to put your blame
Inside your feeling empty
Sick with what I've said
Carved in denial
Starved in blank expression
Starring back at you
It's all caught up to you now
The way you live your life
Who's to say you are wrong

Who's to say anything at all
Who's to say that you're real
No one except your real death sanity trip you play
Closing your eyes will not make the room stop spinning
Will not keep the walls from closing in
It's not that I couldn't stop you
I just wanted to see how it would all turn out
How much everyone really cared
How much they sneered and laughed at you
In disgust for you
In a violence so deep
They actually wanted to hurt you themselves
Run their hands all over your body
As it lays in a casket
They watch you carefully

♦♦♦

I just stood there when I heard the news
I couldn't catch my breath for a moment
I was shocked
To young...way to young
You start looking at your own habits a little
You stare at your own mortality
Just a little
Then you get right back to it
The day to day
Until you hear about the next one
And the next one
Then all of a sudden
You find yourself there
Gasping for that last moment
Trying to hold onto memory
Anything to bring you back
You can never go back
Stay the course
You belong there
Right where you stand
Where ever that is

◆◆◆

I didn't want to talk about it anymore
It had all been said
It had all been not said
There were things I wanted to bring up and things I wanted on the table
But it didn't seem to matter then so I guess it really doesn't matter now
Sometimes the things we really want to say are so bitter and delusional
That we think the other person will think as deeply as you do about the
    situation
They don't
Move on
A grudge not held is a better day ahead
You'll have the moment to seize
It's just not exactly the right time
These things and their reasons have to sometimes present themselves
    awkwardly
Like spinning knifes
Until you grab the exact one you need
To throw or to cut
To kill or to tame
You can never undo aggressive
You can never forget your name

TIMELESS

No idea how old I was
I didn't matter
Time was lost
It's been lost for as long as I remember
It's been an empty feeling
I notice it every once and every while and every day and every night and
    every time I think of you
After I became numb
I became someone I admired
A hero at their own peace
A mirror left standing without the judgement of my own demise
Oh, what have you become
In the shadows and in the light
In the moments left pondering
In the dead at night
I am forever lonely
My judge and my jury
My personal persecution
My endless battle against my former and current self
You know the feeling
The pace the thrill
The hunt
The kill
You know the feeling until it drags you out of your own skin
Then you can't remember
Like it's the first time
So sweet
The taste
The victim
The tide changes
You follow it
You have no choice
Let it kill you
Let everything kill you
Embrace everything so big and so sweet and destined to be the destruction
You know it all too well
Eat it right out of the hands

Don't pretend you won't
Don't say you won't
You always take the biggest bite
The hope is to stay alive
You're so silly to believe
But you do
With foolish ambition
The razors are so sharp
Yet you run and run and run
Good for you
Let everything devour you
Few do
Only the lonely ones do
They will die completely, through and through

◆ ◆ ◆

I was bleeding out
You couldn't save me
All the ways you tried to soak up the way things happened didn't work
I was lifeless
But meaningful in my death
My death to you
My return to normal for me
All the dying makes sense
It helps me breathe again
It's all I know
You wait for it after awhile
You couldn't save me
I'm in love with death

All the Debts

Pain is necessary
Emotional
Physical
It helps in the discovery of truth
I'm conditioned
Year after year
New pains highlight my eyes
Squeezing the last bits of joy
Taking whatever fortitude I have
Killing the scene in which I try to create
I do not fault
I do not blame
I take in stride
Applaud the actions and insanity
Tip my hat to the crowd so to speak
I watch you as you watch me
The tortured scarecrow
Called to the field from the barn to protect the newest crops
Tortured for the rites of spring and good harvest for others
And in all the applause
Back to the waiting
To be called upon again
Yet I have retired
I have shed all fear of the unknown
I've seen it all
The ugliness of truth
A victory I will never have
Myself I go against
I'm fighting the notions
I bet my soul not to love again
Because eventually it hurts beyond measure
The pieces they take
As I approach the middle of my life
I'm exhausted
I've been on the run for so long
So fucking long
But I am an expert runner

Conditioned
Measured and true to a fault
I'll meet you again
Sometime in the spring
So I can die another death

A Mother's Son

There was a moment of truth between us
But it was as passing as the dead hands we both have held
Truces were left broken
Faceless acts of feverish childhood notions remained steady in a dream
I lay here looking up at the promise broken
While death stares back in my direction
I'll leave my apologies in the next room
Wrapped in paper and bow
Glass of wine pours next to
A box of photographs and well thought plans on the table
You can be there
Left in scene
Broken as me
Dying the same breath
Humming the same distant song of regret and isolation
I can never be the same
We can never be the same
I love you
I think of you often

◆◆◆

When the dreaming ended I started to notice
All the outlined fragments of delusion and comfort
We control our emotions with pills and scrutiny
With knives to our throats
We ask for freedom and forgiveness
We let go of the never again and think sometimes maybe

I stood in the rain and watched you from a block away
Your hair flowing in and out of your face
It was like I never seen you before
The first time is always the best
That first taste I took of you
All the closed eyes of passion and embrace
Dying in each other's arms to justify some silly crush
I think about the moment sometimes when I disappear
In other eyes and skin

The touch is never the same
In truth I exhale you out every so often
I break through to this side of me that never shows
But my cravings for the kill tell me more about the hero I never became
   only the victim I've become
My own victim
My own demise
I walk away and pretend we never happened

◆◆◆

I was in my head again
The colors were screaming through the lenses
Images were blurred and starting to resemble memory
I fell to my knees
My arms to their sides
All I could do was look up
My eyes were turning inside themselves
Distant and calm
Threating indifference
I want the defining moment when it all goes away
The room is impossible to find
The fragments of what is left mean something
Pretending
I almost wanted to die
Just like I almost wanted to live
I'm in the middle
With everything so beautiful broken beside me
Come place your hand under my chin and bring me to my feet
Tell me I'm worth it
Lie to me
Just tell me I mater
Lie to me
Just tell me something that means something
I promise I won't believe it
I can't
It seems that only my sorrow brings the memories to the surface
Of what I pretend to be and what I pretend to know

I am a happy person
The depression takes me places and I just ride
Ride and hold on till the brakes come off and I slam into the fucking wall
Then sleep finds me
I crave it
It slows the mind down
Makes me sense the death and timing of things
You have to wait out the pain
Makes you stronger
Makes you remember
Good times
Very few but there
Very difficult because of ending results but all the same
There's still blood on the floor
Just makes sure it's your own

♦♦♦

The memorial is tomorrow
I still don't feel dead
I've played this scene out so many times in my head
I guess everyone does
What happens
Who cares
Who doesn't
What's left
What does everything equal
My life has always been touch and go
Or maybe more like the scene of a tragic accident
Bodies thrown everywhere and I'm sitting on the side of road wondering
     what the fuck just happened
I'm going to miss you
Our talks
Our stories
I'll be in the next room
Always
You can speak about me the same
I'm still here
I'm just a memory but never faded

My burial was never an ending
Just a see you later
Have a pint for me
I'll see you soon

♦♦♦

Many nights blinded by adolescence
Confused of love and dead by reference
Look serious but laugh
Look calm but violent
The skies open up
The rain drowns your senses
Look around
Become yourself

♦♦♦

You made me
You will destroy me
I am yours
But you are also mine
Together
Through this battle of who owns who
You use me
Beat me
Blind me
Stab me
Caress me
Lick me
Fuck me
As you kill me
I'm used to it
I like it
Brings tears to my eyes when you stop
Pleasured pain
Burn me some more
Uncover me in the middle of the night
Wake me to ravage me
It feels good

Tastes like wine
Eagerly waiting to age
Get the point
I love you so much that I let you
Blood on my face
I will always grin
I like the chips stacked against me
I like it when I'm loosing
Let's see who wins the war
Who can last longer
Me or you
Do your best
Please
I like it
Kill me some more

♦♦♦

You wanted to see it live
Almost to point where it could breath
Then the throat gets slit
The aftermath is always fresh to clean
How vulnerable it is to ascertain and diminish
The value and charismatic behavior
Making the whole thing twist and turn
Like the knife inside the belly
Searching for the lime light
Searching for the truth

Truth flows like a river these days
Unfortunately it empties in to the valley less divine
Mostly on the tongues of cruel behavior
We look up and close our eyes

In the disgust and in between
In the moment gone and forgotten
Is where the days seem to turn and ache
Yesterdays are not the same anymore
The todays swallow the meaning

I like the taste
My river of truth has played the echoes of time on my face
Feature after feature
Live and in plain view
To you I apologize
For my plague is simple
My distaste is pure at heart
My eyes close easy these days
I have peace in my life at last
An open wound now leaves its scar
I'm more relaxed with it now
More at ease to lending discomfort
I have found a solace all my own
I have found a trust to spill into
Pour my guts out and in return receive the same
She will never make me a victim against myself
Me my worst enemy
My favorite villain
I can finally say I'm ok

◆◆◆

I want to be asleep
Closed off
Only the echoes of yesterday serving as a memory
Mind erased
Eased to the point of retire behind my eyes
Heavily shut
Conditioned to exhaust
Wander the endless realm of dreams
Confusion in waking and dying
Let me finish the dream before I wake to the nightmare
Let me replace the morbid reality with a desperate taste of illusion
I need to betray my mind

I'm not what I gave you
But it was everything
All of it
Never some
Never less

In the end of things
I just want to know that I put everything on the table
Even my sanity
Even my weapons

Some of Us Love You

She was poised for greatness
With arrows in her skin
Like spring
In a summer shell
A Cupid's taste for daring adventure
The lick of tongue and sweat that followed
Each day unfolded something naive
Something soft to touch
Immunity and closure
Obscurity and trust
Clouds rolled inside her eyes
Heaven parted ways with her long before
She became involved
Evolution was a pace
Her distinction was a curse
Plagued regret at every turn
My eyes fixated on her movement
I could recite every word it spoke
Telling me this
Telling me that
Long distance runner I became
Yet I never knew to where
I just kept going
Till my knees broke down
Till my body bled
I kept punching air until the motions made sense
Enough for me to embrace
Enough for me to retaliate against myself
For you see
Some of us Love you
Some of us don't
Some of us Hunt you
Some of us won't
Was I looking for you till dawn tasted dusk
Was I spiraling you in my mind
Making you real
Making you a God

To which I could clench my good favors in my teeth
While you watched me beg and beg
I pleaded for Death
Some of us want the End so bad
But it never comes
It always notions us
Greets us heavy at the door
Then says goodbye
Some of us are here because we just can't see it through
To the other side of the door
Where's there's a reckoning we aren't prepared for
Where there's a plate of food warm to the touch and cold to the taste
In which you devour your own soul to be brave enough to exhaust the
    motion
Open mouth screaming
In any direction that will listen
Your heart has broken many times
It will never be a last time
Until the beat stops
The Rhythm of Decline
The song and dance
Some of us love you
Some of us hate ourselves

To be continued…